WORLD CUP EXPERT

PLAYERS

Pete May

W

FRANKLIN WATTS
LONDON • SYDNEY

First published in 2013 by
Franklin Watts
338 Euston Road
London
NW1 3BH

Franklin Watts Australia
Level 17/207 Kent Street
Sydney
NSW 2000

HB ISBN 978 1 4451 2372 1
Library eBook ISBN 978 14451 2374 5
Dewey number: 796.3'34668

A CIP catalogue record for this book is
available from the British Library.

Series Editor: Julia Bird
Series Design: d–r–ink.com

Picture credits: AFP/Getty Images: 9, 14. Allstar Picture Library/Alamy: 26.
Atgimages/Dreamstime: 5b. Gabriel Bouys/AFP/Getty Images: 25t.
Clive Brunskill/Getty Images: 19b. EPA/Alamy: 27b. The FA/via Getty Images: 27t.
Getty Images: 1, 16. Keystone/Hulton Archive/Getty Images: 8. Toshifumi Kitamura/AFP/Getty
Images: 21. Yiannis Kourtoglou/Shutterstock: 4. Maxisport/Shutterstock: 20. Eoghan McNally/
Shutterstock: 23. Natursports/Shutterstock: 24. Offside Sports Photography: 7.
Popperfoto/Getty Images: front cover, 6. Art Rickerby/Time Life Pictures/Getty Images: 5t.
Jean–Yves Ruszniewski/TempSport/Corbis: 18. Peter Schols/AFP/Getty Images: 22c.
Javier Soriano/AFP/Getty Images: 25b. Rick Stewart/Getty Images: 17b.
STF/AFP/Getty Images: 10, 28b. Bob Thomas/Getty Images: 11, 12, 13, 15t, 17t, 29b.

Printed in China

Franklin Watts is a division of
Hachette Children's Books, an Hachette UK company.
www.hachette.co.uk

CONTENTS

THE WORLD CUP

The FIFA World Cup is a month-long celebration of football which is held every four years. Teams from 32 countries battle it out on the pitch for the ultimate prize in football – the World Cup trophy.

Winning the World Cup is the crowning moment of any football player's career.

GREAT PLAYERS

What makes a great World Cup player? Some stars will always stand out. Brazil's Pelé dominated the 1970 World Cup. It was the first time a World Cup had been seen on colour TV and Brazil's football seemed as bright as their yellow shirts. Diego Maradona propelled Argentina to World Cup glory in 1986 through a combination of genius and streetwise cunning. Johan Cruyff only finished with a runners-up medal in 1974, but gave his name to the 'Cruyff turn' and treated the world to the first display of 'total football'.

GREAT GOALS

Goalscorers win tournaments, which is why Brazil's Ronaldo makes the top ten, as does Germany's Jürgen Klinsmann, who scored three or more goals in three successive tournaments. But there are other considerations to be made in selecting the greatest World Cup players. Creative genius sees Zinedine Zidane and Andrés Iniesta in the top rank. Longevity has to be a factor, which is why Germany's Lothar Matthäus is included, as he is the only player ever to feature in five tournaments.

WORLD CUP FAST FACTS

FOUNDED: 1930

NUMBER OF TEAMS THAT TAKE PART: 32 (expanded from 16 in 1978 and again from 24 in 1982)

MOST SUCCESSFUL TEAM: Brazil

TOP GOAL-SCORER: Ronaldo (15)

FORMAT: For the group stage, teams are put in eight groups of four teams. Each team plays all the other three teams once. The top two teams from each group qualify for the knock-out stages, where the winner of one group plays the runner-up of another. The winners of this qualify for the eight-team quarter-finals, which are followed by the semi-finals and the long-awaited World Cup final itself.

LEADERS

Leadership is vital for every side, and Bobby Moore inspired his men through his unflappable approach. He was an immaculate defender, but also managed to make two goals for England in the 1966 World Cup final. Age is also a factor and to win the World Cup at 40, as Italy's goalkeeper and captain Dino Zoff did, is a fantastic achievement.

UP FOR DEBATE

This selection will always be controversial. Players who can count themselves unlucky not to make the top ten include Hungary's star of 1954, Ferenc Puskás, West Germany's heroes of 1974, Franz Beckenbauer and Gerd Müller, and England's 1966 hat-trick legend Geoff Hurst. But hopefully readers will agree on one thing, all ten players in this book have, in many different ways, contributed to the magic of the World Cup.

Pelé's amazing skills lit up four World Cup tournaments.

This statue of Bobby Moore, one of England's greatest ever players, stands outside Wembley Stadium in London.

BOBBY MOORE

BOBBY MOORE

FAST FACTS

DATE OF BIRTH: 12 April 1941 [died 24 February 1993]

PLACE OF BIRTH: Barking

COUNTRY REPRESENTED: England

POSITION: Central defender

WORLD CUPS PLAYED IN: 1962, 1966, 1970

CLUBS PLAYED FOR: West Ham, Fulham, San Antonio Thunder, Seattle Sounders, Herning Fremad

'My captain, my leader, my right-hand man. He was the spirit and the heartbeat of the team.'

Sir Alf Ramsey, England manager

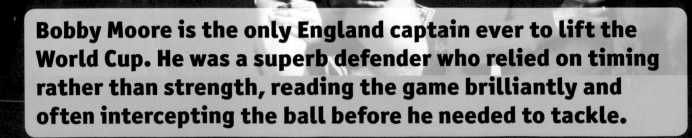

Bobby Moore is the only England captain ever to lift the World Cup. He was a superb defender who relied on timing rather than strength, reading the game brilliantly and often intercepting the ball before he needed to tackle.

GOAL MAGIC

Moore played in the 1962 World Cup in Chile, and in all six games of England's 1966 World Cup triumph. He made England's first goal in the World Cup final against West Germany with a chipped free kick to his West Ham team mate Geoff Hurst, who headed the ball powerfully into the goal. Moore also made England's fourth and decisive goal in the last minute of extra-time with a beautiful long ball out of defence to Hurst, who crashed the ball into the top corner of the net. The image of the clean-cut, blond-haired Moore lifting the Jules Rimet trophy entered English folklore.

TESTING TIMES

Moore's cool, unflappable image was tested in the 1970 World Cup in Mexico. He was accused of stealing a bracelet from a jewellery shop in Bogotá, Colombia, arrested by police and placed under house arrest for four days, before all charges were dropped. Moore went on to play in all England's games and gave a superb performance in the 1–0 group game defeat by Brazil. His precisely timed challenge on the powerful winger Jairzinho was hailed as the perfect tackle, and the Brazilian football legend Pelé (see pages 8–9) described Moore as the best defender he had ever played against.

NATIONAL HERO

Moore played his last international match in 1973, having won a then record 108 caps for his country. When Moore died of cancer in 1993 there was a national outpouring of grief and thousands of scarves were placed in a shrine at the gates of his old club West Ham United. A statue of Moore now stands outside Wembley Stadium (see page 5).

Bobby Moore and Pelé swapped shirts at the end of their group match to show their mutual respect.

DID YOU KNOW?

Moore almost didn't play in the 1966 World Cup because he was out of contract at West Ham and technically ineligible. Only the intervention of manager Sir Alf Ramsey persuaded him to sign a contract on the eve of the tournament.

'Before the match, I told myself that Pelé was just flesh and bones like the rest of us. Later I realised I'd been wrong.'

Tarcisio Burgnich, Italy defender

Pelé

FAST FACTS

DATE OF BIRTH: 23 October 1940

PLACE OF BIRTH: Três Corações

COUNTRY REPRESENTED: Brazil

POSITION: Striker

WORLD CUPS PLAYED IN: 1958, 1962, 1966, 1970

CLUBS PLAYED FOR: Santos, New York Cosmos

Edson Arantes do Nascimento, better known as Pelé, was the brightest star in a Brazil team packed full of talent and flair.

EARLY SUCCESS

Pelé made his international debut at just 16, and in 1958 at 17 years and 249 days old he was the then youngest player to play in a World Cup (Northern Ireland's Norman Whiteside later broke his record). He scored a hat trick in the semi-final win over France and two goals in the 1958 World Cup final – a brilliant 5–2 victory against Sweden – including a superb chip over a defender and a volley into the net. After scoring in the first match of the 1962 World Cup, Pelé was injured and missed Brazil's victory.

WORLD CLASS

Pelé will always be best remembered for his brilliant performances for Brazil at the 1970 World Cup. He scored with a header in the final against Italy and made the decisive pass for Brazil's fourth goal scored by Carlos Alberto in a memorable 4–1 victory. This final goal was the result of wonderful passing by Brazil, with eight players involved in the move, and is often described as the greatest goal in World Cup history. Pelé scored a total of four goals in the tournament, nearly netted from the halfway line against Czechoslovakia and inspired England's goalkeeper Gordon Banks to make the best save of his career.

GREATEST TEAM

Pelé became the first player to score in three successive World Cups in 1966, but threatened never to play in a World Cup again after being injured by tough tackling as Brazil failed to qualify from the group stage. Thankfully he went back on his threat in 1970, and became the talisman for the creative flair and 'Samba football' of Brazil's greatest side. For many people, he is the greatest player of all time.

DID YOU KNOW?

Pelé had a part in the 1981 film 'Escape To Victory' along with Bobby Moore, Sylvester Stallone and Michael Caine. He plays a prisoner in a World War Two camp who escapes during an exhibition football match against Germany.

Pelé was an unbelievable talent on the pitch, forcing the opposition into fouls and clumsy tackles.

'We showed the world you could enjoy being a footballer, you could laugh and have a fantastic time. I represent the era which proved that attractive football was enjoyable and successful.'

Johan Cruyff

Johan Cruyff

Johan Cruyff was a striker, but could pop up anywhere on the pitch. His ball skills were mesmerising and he invented 'the Cruyff turn' against Sweden, a feint and drag back that left defenders floundering.

GREAT GOALIE

Zoff was an imposing figure. At 1.8 metres, he wasn't tall for a goalkeeper, but he more than made up for it with his athleticism and huge hands. He made superb reaction saves and was an intimidating presence in a one-on-one situation. His air of calm inspired the resolute Italian defence.

WAITING GAME

Zoff was in the squad for the 1970 Mexico World Cup, but had to be content with a reserve role. By 1974 he was the first choice goalkeeper and played in all three group games as Italy went out of the tournament on goal difference. It was in the first group game that Haiti ended Zoff's astonishing record of 1,142 minutes without conceding a goal for Italy. At the 1978 World Cup Zoff was named team captain, a rare honour for a goalkeeper. He kept a clean sheet as Italy beat the eventual winners Argentina in the group stage and was unlucky to see his side miss out on the final after losing to the Netherlands. He was criticised for letting in Arie Haan's long-range shot and some said his reflexes were slowing.

GLORY AT LAST

But the 1982 World Cup was to belong to Zoff, the man nicknamed 'The Monument of Italian Football'. He kept another clean sheet in the semi-final win against Poland, and, in the second round game against Brazil, produced a great late save from Oscar's header as Italy beat the tournament favourites 3–2. He produced another crucial block while Italy were one goal up in the final against West Germany. The Italians went on to win the final 3–1. The sight of a 40-year-old in a goalkeeper's jersey lifting the World Cup trophy is one of the greatest World Cup moments.

'Dino was Italy's most important player in 1982. He was the one who truly represented the team. He was an example to all of us, myself more than anyone.'

Paolo Rossi,
Italy striker

Dino Zoff proudly displays the World Cup trophy to the crowd and press.

DID YOU KNOW?

Zoff came from a family of farmers. He joked: 'If I weren't a goalkeeper I couldn't be anything else but a farmer with the hands I've got.'

Matthäus makes a vital tackle on Maradona in the 1986 World Cup final.

Lothar Matthäus

Lothar Matthäus is the only outfield player to participate in five World Cups. He was an inspirational box-to-box midfielder for most of his career, who could both tackle and create with defence-splitting passes.

FAST FACTS

DATE OF BIRTH: 21 March 1961

PLACE OF BIRTH: Erlangen

COUNTRIES REPRESENTED: West Germany and Germany

POSITION: Midfield or defence

WORLD CUPS PLAYED IN: 1982, 1986, 1990, 1994, 1998

CLUBS PLAYED FOR: Borussia Mönchengladbach, Bayern Munich, Inter Milan, MetroStars

DID YOU KNOW?

Matthäus's nickname was 'Der Terminator', after the Arnold Schwarzenegger character, because of his strength and ruthlessness.

EARLY DAYS

Matthäus appeared in the 1982 World Cup aged 21, making two substitute appearances as West Germany reached the final. He was an unused sub as West Germany lost the final to Italy. In the 1986 World Cup tournament, Matthäus scored against Morocco in the group stage, as West Germany went on to reach the final. He performed a fine man-to-man marking job on Argentine legend Diego Maradona (see pages 16–17) in the final, which West Germany lost 3–2. Maradona later described Matthäus as his toughest opponent.

FINEST HOUR

The 1990 World Cup saw Matthäus's finest achievement as he captained West Germany to victory in their third successive final. The final was a re-match against Argentina, won through Andreas Brehme's late penalty. Matthäus had a great tournament, scoring four goals, including two against Yugoslavia in their group clash. Matthäus became the last captain to lift the trophy for West Germany before its reunification with East Germany later in 1990.

INTO THE HISTORY BOOKS

In the 1994 World Cup Matthäus moved back to a sweeper role, and captained Germany to the quarter-finals, scoring a penalty as the side lost to Bulgaria. No one expected him to appear in the 1998 World Cup at the age of 37, but it was always dangerous to write off Matthäus. He was called into the squad as a late replacement for the injured Mattias Sammer and played in four matches to become the most capped German player ever.

DIEGO MARADONA

FAST FACTS

DATE OF BIRTH: 30 October 1960

PLACE OF BIRTH: Lanús, Buenos Aires

COUNTRY REPRESENTED: Argentina

POSITION: Attacking midfielder, second striker

WORLD CUPS PLAYED IN: 1982, 1986, 1990, 1994

CLUBS PLAYED FOR: Argentinos Juniors, Boca Juniors, Barcelona, Napoli, Sevilla, Newell's Old Boys, Boca Juniors

Diego Maradona was a tremendously skilful forward for Argentina, who grew up in poverty in Buenos Aires. With his low centre of gravity and superb dribbling and passing, Maradona was considered to be the best player in the world in the 1980s.

HAND OF GOD

Always controversial, Maradona scored twice in the 1982 World Cup, but was sent off against Brazil. He is best remembered for the contrasting goals he scored against England in the 1986 World Cup quarter-final in Mexico. For his first, he punched the ball over England's goalkeeper Peter Shilton. The referee believed Maradona had headed the ball and the goal stood. Maradona later said the goal was 'a little with the head of Maradona and a little with the Hand of God'. The expression stuck.

GENIUS GOALS

Maradona's second goal was one of the best individual goals ever seen as he sprinted from his own half, taking 11 touches and beating five England players before rounding Shilton to score. It is often described as the goal of the century. In the semi-final, a 3–2 win against Belgium, Maradona scored twice, including another superb solo effort. In the final against West Germany he laid on the pass for the winning goal in a thrilling 3–2 victory. The

genius of Maradona had propelled an average Argentina team to World Cup glory.

TROUBLED TIMES

Despite being hampered by an ankle injury during the 1990 World Cup, Maradona still set up the goal that helped Argentina reach the final, where they lost to a late goal by West Germany's Andreas Brehme. Maradona was in tears at the final whistle.

THE END

By the 1994 World Cup Maradona's lifestyle was increasingly chaotic. He played twice in the 1994 World Cup, scoring a memorable goal against Greece and running to the camera with a wild-eyed stare. After the match he tested positive for using ephedrine, a performance-enhancing drug. Maradona was never to play international football again as his incredible career of 91 games and 34 goals ended in disgrace.

The infamous 'Hand of God' goal.

DID YOU KNOW?

As a child Maradona fell into a pit of sewage and nearly drowned before being saved by his Uncle Cirilo.

Maradona sprints to celebrate with his team mates after scoring against Greece at the 1994 World Cup.

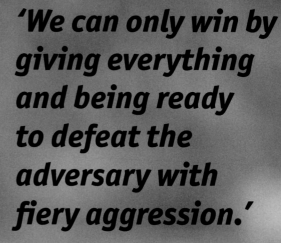

'We can only win by giving everything and being ready to defeat the adversary with fiery aggression.'

Jürgen Klinsmann

Jürgen Klinsmann

FAST FACTS

DATE OF BIRTH: 30 July 1964

PLACE OF BIRTH: Göppingen

COUNTRY REPRESENTED: West Germany, Germany

POSITION: Striker

WORLD CUPS PLAYED IN: 1990, 1994, 1998

CLUBS PLAYED FOR: VfB Stuttgart, Inter Milan, Monaco, Tottenham Hotspur, Bayern Munich, Sampdoria, Orange County Blue Star

Jürgen Klinsmann was one of Germany's greatest ever marksmen. The blond striker scored 11 goals in 17 World Cup games and was the first player to score three goals or more in three successive World Cups.

FANTASTIC FINISHER

Klinsmann was superb at getting in front of his marker and could finish with diving headers, volleys and precise shots. The highlight of his career was winning the 1990 World Cup with West Germany. He scored three goals in the tournament, including a typical near post finish for the vital first goal against the Netherlands in the last 16 round, a great flicked header against Yugoslavia and another header versus the United Arab Emirates in the group games.

QUICK EXIT

Klinsmann scored five times at the 1994 World Cup for the reunified Germany side, even though Germany unexpectedly lost to Bulgaria in the quarter-final. Possibly the best goal of his career was his flick-up and turn for a stunning volley against South Korea.

CAPTAIN KLINSMANN

Although the German side was ageing in the 1998 World Cup, Klinsmann as captain again showed his class with three very different goals: showing great control before volleying home against the USA, scoring with a diving header after the ball rebounded off the post against Iran, and a poached effort against Mexico. He went on to manage an acclaimed Germany team at the 2006 World Cup and is currently the manager of the USA.

DID YOU KNOW?

When Klinsmann made his debut for Tottenham Hotspur in 1994, he celebrated scoring at Sheffield Wednesday by making an exaggerated dive to mock claims that he went down too easily when tackled.

Klinsmann is tackled by Igor Štimac of Croatia during their 1998 quarter-final clash.

'To hold the World
Cup in my hands
is one of the
most incredible
moments of
my life.'

Ronaldo

RONALDO

DID YOU KNOW?

Ronaldo's weight
ballooned after
retiring. In 2012
he starred in a TV
weight-loss reality
show, losing 17 kg
through, among
other exercises,
dancing to the
Gangnam Style
video!

**Brazil's Ronaldo was said to be the world's
most complete striker — a fantastic
dribbler and instinctive finisher who scored
a record 15 goals in World Cup tournaments.**

FINAL HEARTBREAK

When Brazil reached the 1998 World Cup final in Paris, Ronaldo had already scored four times, including a great effort off the outside of his boot against Morocco and Brazil's goal in the 1–1 draw with the Netherlands in the semi-final. He also converted the vital first penalty in the semi-final shoot-out win. But the world was stunned when Ronaldo suffered a mysterious fit on the eve of the final and was first left off the Brazil team sheet, then reinstated just half an hour before kick-off. He was clearly not fit to play the match and France went on to win 3–0.

GOAL MACHINE

Ronaldo erased that unhappy memory by scoring both Brazil's goals in the 2002 World Cup final against Germany. That big smile returned as he first pounced on a rebound off Oliver Kahn the German keeper, then produced a precise finish from the edge of the box. He scored eight goals in the tournament and won the Golden Boot as top scorer. His tally included a goal from a seemingly impossible angle against Costa Rica and a lovely shot with the outside of his right boot to win the semi-final against Turkey.

FITNESS AND FORM

Ronaldo scored a hat-trick of penalties against Argentina in a qualifying match for the 2006 World Cup, but was criticised by some for being overweight at the tournament. He still scored twice against Japan and once against Ghana, his record-breaking 15th World Cup goal featuring a typically nonchalant dummy to round the goalkeeper and score.

Ronaldo does his trademark finger-wagging celebration after scoring the first goal in the 2002 World Cup final.

FAST FACTS

DATE OF BIRTH: 22 September 1976

PLACE OF BIRTH: Rio de Janeiro

COUNTRY REPRESENTED: Brazil

POSITION: Striker

WORLD CUPS PLAYED IN: 1998, 2002, 2006

CLUBS PLAYED FOR: Cruzeiro, PSV Eindhoven, Barcelona, Inter Milan, Real Madrid, AC Milan, Corinthians

ZINEDINE ZIDANE

Zinedine Zidane was a magician of a midfielder. He could find space and make passes from seemingly impossible angles.

FRENCH HERO

Born to French Algerian parents in Marseille, Zidane opted to play for France and did much to promote racial unity in the country. In the 1998 World Cup, his two headed goals helped win the final for France as they beat Brazil 3–0 in Paris. Zidane had been instrumental in France's run to the final. He became a national hero and his image was projected onto the famous Arc de Triomphe after France won the Cup.

MIDFIELD MAESTRO

Injury kept Zidane out of all but one of France's games at the 2002 World Cup as the holders crashed out at the group stage in a memorable tournament upset. Two years later, in 2004, Zidane announced his retirement from international football. But it was to be shortlived, as Zidane returned to Les Bleus to help inspire France to the World Cup final in 2006, setting up the winning goal against Brazil in the quarter-final and scoring the winner with a penalty against Portugal in the semi-final.

CLOSE GAME

Having announced he was to retire once more from football after the final, most neutrals were willing on Zidane to win another World Cup winners' medal. He scored with an audacious chipped penalty after seven minutes, only for Marco Materazzi to equalise for Italy. When the game went into extra-time Zidane almost won it for France as Buffon made a brilliant save to tip over his header.

MOMENT OF MADNESS

Then with ten minutes of extra-time left, came an astonishing moment. In an off-the-ball incident Zidane headbutted Marco Materazzi in the chest and was sent off. The world speculated what Materazzi had said to provoke such a reaction. Materazzi later admitted that he had insulted Zidane's sister. Despite the red card and France going on to lose to Italy on penalties, Zidane still received a rousing welcome home in France. If anything the incident cemented his love affair with the nation.

'Playing for the team has given me my greatest satisfaction, my greatest joy.'

Zinedine Zidane, on playing for the French national team

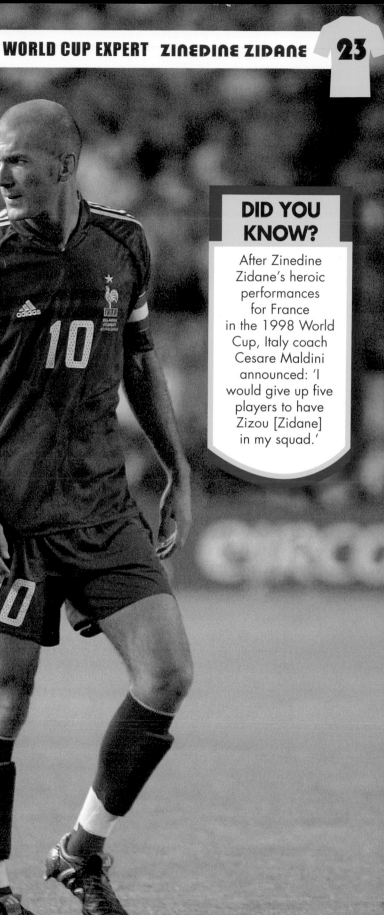

DID YOU KNOW?

After Zinedine Zidane's heroic performances for France in the 1998 World Cup, Italy coach Cesare Maldini announced: 'I would give up five players to have Zizou [Zidane] in my squad.'

FAST FACTS

DATE OF BIRTH: 23 June 1972

PLACE OF BIRTH: Marseille

COUNTRY REPRESENTED: France

POSITION: Attacking midfield

WORLD CUPS PLAYED IN: 1998, 2002, 2006

CLUBS PLAYED FOR: Cannes, Bordeaux, Juventus, Real Madrid

'I don't play the game to be number one. I play to be happy.'

ANDRÉS INIESTA

Andrés Iniesta is the mastermind behind the 'tiki taka' passing game of Spain. His game relies upon superb balance, his feel for the ball, quick feet and a tremendous range of flicks and feints.

DID YOU KNOW?

Iniesta keeps every pair of boots that he has played in, including his first boots, a pair of size eight Adidas Predators.

Iniesta scores an extraordinary extra-time goal in the 2010 World Cup Final.

FAST FACTS

DATE OF BIRTH: 11 May 1984

PLACE OF BIRTH: Fuentealbilla

COUNTRY REPRESENTED: Spain

POSITION: Attacking midfielder

WORLD CUPS PLAYED IN: 2006, 2010

CLUBS PLAYED FOR: Barcelona

MIDFIELD MASTER

Iniesta plays at the heart of the most successful Spanish national team of all time, forming an instinctive partnership with midfielder Xavi. Although he is a relatively slight figure, Iniesta is very difficult to take the ball off once he goes on a dribble.

WORLD CUP WIZARD

Iniesta was in the Spain squad for the 2006 World Cup, playing just once before they were knocked out of the tournament 3–1 by France in the second round. However, the highlight of Iniesta's career so far has undoubtedly been scoring the winning goal for Spain in the 2010 World Cup Final against the Netherlands in Johannesburg. He scored in the 116th minute, four minutes from the end of extra-time, just as a penalty shoot-out appeared inevitable. Found by Barcelona team mate Cesc Fabregas on the edge of the box, Iniesta waited for the ball to drop before sending an expert half-volley past the Dutch goalkeeper, Stekelenburg. He whipped off his shirt, revealing a white vest with a tribute to Dani Jarque, a former youth player who died of a heart attack in 2009. Iniesta was named man of the match in the final.

Match-winner Iniesta grabs the trophy as Spain wins the World Cup for the first time.

SPANISH SKILLS

What makes Iniesta almost the complete footballer is his ability to play anywhere, though his best position is as an attacking midfielder. A product of Barcelona's youth system and a modest man off the pitch, Iniesta has completed a tremendous international treble through winning not only the 2010 World Cup, but also the 2008 and 2012 European Championships with Spain.

STARS OF THE FUTURE

Football is always looking out for the next Pelé or Maradona, especially at World Cup tournaments. Here are just a few players who may light up the World Cup in the future.

NEYMAR (BRAZIL)

Tagged 'the next Pelé' by some, the Brazil striker has huge potential and scored more than a hundred goals at Santos before joining Barcelona. A great dribbler and finisher, Neymar can score both short and long-range goals. His flicks, backheels, stepovers and choreographed celebrations (plus his sometimes Mohican hairstyle and an earring) will surely enliven the World Cup for years to come.

JACK WILSHERE (ENGLAND)

The Arsenal midfielder could solve England's problem of keeping possession of the ball. He dictates the pace of a game and rarely wastes a pass. Wilshere is a fine tackler too. A player with great creative vision, he might just be the player England can build a team around – if he can stay fit.

RADAMEL FALCAO (COLOMBIA)

The Colombia and Monaco striker is able to score from just about any angle with both feet and head. Nicknamed El Tigre (The Tiger), he could be a World Cup star for in-form Colombia. Falcao appears to be the complete striker and has a goal-to-minutes ratio comparable to Messi and Ronaldo. He can score after mazy dribbles or wlth stunning overhead kicks, volleys and headers.

WORLD CUP

1. Bobby Moore, the captain of England's 1966 World Cup-winning side played for which English side?

a) Manchester United
b) Liverpool
c) West Ham United

2. After his two goals helped France win the 1998 World Cup, the image of Zinedine Zidane was projected onto what iconic French structure?

a) The Eiffel Tower
b) The Arc de Triomphe
c) Notre Dame

3.) Whom did Maradona score his 'Hand of God' goal against in 1986?

a) Belgium
b) West Germany
c) England

4. How old was Italy goalkeeper Dino Zoff when he picked up the 1982 World Cup?

a) 40
b) 41
c) 39

5. How many World Cups did Germany's Lothar Matthäus play in?

a) Four
b) Five
c) Three

6. Johan Cruyff lent his name to 'the Cruyff turn' after a dummy against which side in the 1974 World Cup?

a) West Germany
b) Argentina
c) Sweden

7. What happened to Brazil's Ronaldo on the eve of the 1998 World Cup final?

a) He suffered a groin strain
b) He broke his metatarsal bone
c) He suffered a fit

8. Pelé made the decisive pass for Brazil's fourth goal in the 1970 World Cup final. Who scored it?

a) Jairzinho
b) Carlos Alberto
c) Rivelino

9. Who was the goalkeeper that Maradona rounded when scoring 'the goal of the century' in the 1986 World Cup?

a) Peter Shilton
b) Harald Schumacher
c) Ray Clemence

10. Which English team did German striker Jürgen Klinsmann once play for?

a) Arsenal
b) Tottenham Hotspur
c) Manchester City

EXPERT QUIZ

11. When Andrés Iniesta scored the winner for Spain in the 2010 World Cup final, he revealed a vest with a slogan. Was it?

a) An advertisement for a Spanish bank
b) A tribute to a Spanish youth player who had died
c) A message thanking God

12. When Zinedine Zidane was sent off in the 2006 World Cup final, was it for?

a) Pushing the referee
b) Biting an opponent
c) Headbutting an opponent

13. In the 1966 World Cup final Bobby Moore's long pass released which player to score England's fourth goal?

a) Geoff Hurst
b) Roger Hunt
c) Martin Peters

14. Johan Cruyff helped create a particular style of football for the Netherlands in 1974. Was it?

a) Total football
b) Tiki taka
c) Route one

15. How old was Pelé when he made his international debut?

a) 18
b) 17
c) 16

16. How many goals did Brazil's Ronaldo score in the 2002 World Cup?

a) Six
b) Eight
c) Seven

17. What was the nickname of Germany's Lothar Matthäus?

a) Der Bomber
b) Der Terminator
c) Der Kaiser

18. Argentina's Maradona made the winning goal against West Germany in the 1986 World Cup final. But who scored it?

a) Brown
b) Burruchaga
c) Valdano

19. Bobby Moore was said to have made the perfect tackle against Brazil in the 1970 World Cup. Who was it he tackled?

a) Pelé
b) Gerson
c) Jairzinho

20. Spain's Iniesta scored the winner in the 2010 World Cup final against the Netherlands. In what city was the game played?

a) Johannesburg
b) Cape Town
c) Pretoria

Answers: 1) c 2) b 3) c 4) a 5) b 6) c 7) c 8) c 9) b 10) a 11) b 12) c 13) c 14) a 15) c 16) b 17) b 18) b 19) b 20) a

GLOSSARY

Ball: Another word for a pass, i.e. a long ball, short ball, etc.

Cap: When you award someone a cap in football, you pick them to play for their country.

Central defender: Someone who plays in the middle of the defence, defending the goal area directly in front of the goalkeeper.

Chip: A pass or shot that is kicked high up in the air, but then descends to its intended target.

Clean sheet: Not conceding any goals.

Cruyff turn: A move made popular by Johan Cruyff in 1974. It involves a dummy and drag back of the ball that deceives a defender.

Debut: A player's first appearance is known as making a debut.

Diving header: A header that is made while diving full length to reach the ball.

Extra-time: A period of 30 extra minutes that is played if a knock-out game is a draw at the end of the standard 90 minutes.

Feint: Where a player uses their body to look as if they are going one way, but then go another.

Fit: A sudden violent attack that can be accompanied by convulsions and may make you fall unconscious.

Free kick: This is awarded when a player is fouled. The fouled team is given a free kick at the ball with no opposition player allowed within ten yards (9.1 metres) of them.

Half-volley: A shot taken when the ball has bounced once.

Hat trick: When a player scores three goals it is said to be a hat-trick.

Intercept: This involves anticipating a pass by the opposition and taking the ball before it reaches its intended target.

Neutral: Someone who doesn't support either of the two teams playing.

Outfield player: Any player who is not a goalkeeper.

Overhead kick: Kicking a high ball over the back of your head with both legs off the ground and one leg higher than the other in a kind of 'scissor' movement. Also known as a bicycle kick.

Performance-enhancing: A drug that improves a player's performance is known as performance–enhancing.

Reaction save: A save relying on the quick reflexes of the goalkeeper.

Striker: A forward who plays close to the opposition goal and whose main purpose is to score goals.

Sweeper: A defender who 'sweeps' up the danger, playing behind one or two centre backs. The sweeper can also move forward when there is the chance to attack.

Talisman: A player of vital importance to a side, who also brings luck and confidence to the other players.

Tiki taka: The short-passing style of play made famous by the Spain football team.

Total football: A fluid style of play created by the Netherlands side of 1974, involving players skilful enough to swap positions.

Volley: A shot taken when the ball is off the ground.

Youth system: A training school for young players, usually attached to a particular football club.

WORLD CUP WINNERS TABLE

Year	Winners	Final score	Runners-up	Venue	Location
1930	Uruguay	4–2	Argentina	Estadio Centenario	Montevideo, Uruguay
1934	Italy	2–1	Czechoslovakia	Stadio Nazionale PNF	Rome, Italy
1938	Italy	4–2	Hungary	Stade Olympique de Colombes	Paris, France
1950	Uruguay	2–1	Brazil	Estádio do Maracanã	Rio de Janeiro, Brazil
1954	West Germany	3–2	Hungary	Wankdorf Stadium	Bern, Switzerland
1958	Brazil	5–2	Sweden	Råsunda Stadium	Solna, Sweden
1962	Brazil	3–1	Czechoslovakia	Estadio Nacional	Santiago, Chile
1966	England	4–2	West Germany	Wembley Stadium	London, England
1970	Brazil	4–1	Italy	Estadio Azteca	Mexico City, Mexico
1974	West Germany	2–1	Netherlands	Olympiastadio	Munich, West Germany
1978	Argentina	3–1	Netherlands	Estadio Monumental	Buenos Aires, Argentina
1982	Italy	3–1	West Germany	Santiago Bernabéu	Madrid, Spain
1986	Argentina	3–2	West Germany	Estadio Azteca	Mexico City, Mexico
1990	West Germany	1–0	Argentina	Stadio Olimpico	Rome, Italy
1994	Brazil	0–0 (3–2 on penalties)	Italy	Rose Bowl	Pasadena, California, USA
1998	France	3–0	Brazil	Stade de France	Saint-Denis, France
2002	Brazil	2–0	Germany	International Stadium	Yokohama, Japan
2006	Italy	1–1	France	Olympiastadion	Berlin, Germany
2010	Spain	1–0	Netherlands	Soccer City	Johannesburg, South Africa

FURTHER INFORMATION

WEB LINKS

http://www.bbc.co.uk/sport/0/football/21317369
Watch Bobby Moore's 'perfect tackle' on Jairzinho (1970)

http://www.youtube.com/watch?v=0HrjevD2vhk
Brazil's wonderful team goal (1970)

http://www.youtube.com/watch?v=U1k7DGqRF5g
The famous Cruyff turn (1974)

http://www.youtube.com/watch?v=ATfjrnet_Dk
Klinsmann's goal against South Korea (1994)

http://news.bbc.co.uk/sport1/hi/football/world_
cup_2010/8808966.stm
Iniesta wins the World Cup (2010)

BOOKS

Foul Football: Wicked World Cup, Michael Coleman (Scholastic, 2010)
Inside Sport: World Cup Football, Clive Gifford (Wayland, 2010)
The World Cup: World Cup 2010, Michael Hurley (Heinemann, 2010)

INDEX